William S. Hunter

Hunter's Panoramic Guide from Niagara Falls to Quebec

William S. Hunter

Hunter's Panoramic Guide from Niagara Falls to Quebec

ISBN/EAN: 9783743443198

Manufactured in Europe, USA, Canada, Australia, Japa

Cover: Foto ©Andreas Hilbeck / pixelio.de

Manufactured and distributed by brebook publishing software (www.brebook.com)

William S. Hunter

Hunter's Panoramic Guide from Niagara Falls to Quebec

**IMAGE EVALUATION
TEST TARGET (MT-3)**

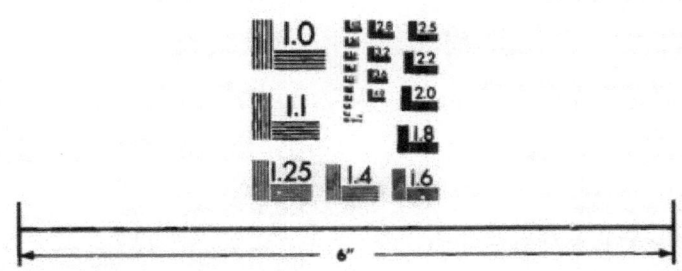

Photographic
Sciences
Corporation

23 WEST MAIN STREET
WEBSTER, N.Y. 14580
(716) 872-4503

Technical and Bibliographic Notes/Notes techniques et bibliographiques

The Institute has attempted to obtain the best original copy available for filming. Features of this copy which may be bibliographically unique, which may alter any of the images in the reproduction, or which may significantly change the usual method of filming, are checked below.

L'Institut a microfilmé le meilleur exemplaire qu'il lui a été possible de se procurer. Les détails de cet exemplaire qui sont peut-être uniques du point de vue bibliographique, qui peuvent modifier une image reproduite, ou qui peuvent exiger une modification dans la méthode normale de filmage sont indiqués ci-dessous.

- [ ] Coloured covers/
  Couverture de couleur

- [ ] Covers damaged/
  Couverture endommagée

- [ ] Covers restored and/or laminated/
  Couverture restaurée et/ou pelliculée

- [ ] Cover title missing/
  Le titre de couverture manque

- [ ] Coloured maps/
  Cartes géographiques en couleur

- [ ] Coloured ink (i.e. other than blue or black)/
  Encre de couleur (i.e. autre que bleue ou noire)

- [ ] Coloured plates and/or illustrations/
  Planches et/ou illustrations en couleur

- [ ] Bound with other material/
  Relié avec d'autres documents

- [ ] Tight binding may cause shadows or distortion along interior margin/
  La reliure serrée peut causer de l'ombre ou de la distortion le long de la marge intérieure

- [ ] Blank leaves added during restoration may appear within the text. Whenever possible, these have been omitted from filming/
  Il se peut que certaines pages blanches ajoutées lors d'une restauration apparaissent dans le texte, mais, lorsque cela était possible, ces pages n'ont pas été filmées.

- [ ] Additional comments:/
  Commentaires supplémentaires:

- [ ] Coloured pages/
  Pages de couleur

- [ ] Pages damaged/
  Pages endommagées

- [ ] Pages restored and/or laminated/
  Pages restaurées et/ou pelliculées

- [x] Pages discoloured, stained or foxed/
  Pages décolorées, tachetées ou piquées

- [ ] Pages detached/
  Pages détachées

- [x] Showthrough/
  Transparence

- [ ] Quality of print varies/
  Qualité inégale de l'impression

- [ ] Includes supplementary material/
  Comprend du matériel supplémentaire

- [ ] Only edition available/
  Seule édition disponible

- [ ] Pages wholly or partially obscured by errata slips, tissues, etc., have been refilmed to ensure the best possible image/
  Les pages totalement ou partiellement obscurcies par un feuillet d'errata, une pelure, etc., ont été filmées à nouveau de façon à obtenir la meilleure image possible.

The images appearing here are the best quality possible considering the condition and legibility of the original copy and in keeping with the filming contract specifications.

Original copies in printed paper covers are filmed beginning with the front cover and ending on the last page with a printed or illustrated impression, or the back cover when appropriate. All other original copies are filmed beginning on the first page with a printed or illustrated impression, and ending on the last page with a printed or illustrated impression.

The last recorded frame on each microfiche shall contain the symbol → (meaning "CONTINUED"), or the symbol ▽ (meaning "END"), whichever applies.

Maps, plates, charts, etc., may be filmed at different reduction ratios. Those too large to be entirely included in one exposure are filmed beginning in the upper left hand corner, left to right and top to bottom, as many frames as required. The following diagrams illustrate the method:

Les images suivantes ont été reproduites avec le plus grand soin, compte tenu de la condition et de la netteté de l'exemplaire filmé, et en conformité avec les conditions du contrat de filmage.

Les exemplaires originaux dont la couverture en papier est imprimée sont filmés en commençan' par le premier plat et en terminant soit par la dernière page qui comporte une empreinte d'impression ou d'illustration, soit par le second plat, selon le cas. Tous les autres exemplaires originaux sont filmés en commençant par la première page qui comporte une empreinte d'impression ou d'illustration et en terminant pa la dernière page qui comporte une telle empreinte.

Un des symboles suivants apparaîtra sur la dernière image de chaque microfiche, selon le cas: le symbole → signifie "A SUIVRE", le symbole ▽ signifie "FIN".

Les cartes, planches, tableaux, etc., peuvent êtr filmés à des taux de réduction différents. Lorsque le document est trop grand pour être reproduit en un seul cliché, il est filmé à partir de l'angle supérieur gauche, de gauche à droite, et de haut en bas, en prenant le nombre d'images nécessaire. Les diagrammes suivants illustrent la méthode.

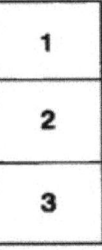

HUNTER'S

PANORAMIC GUIDE

FROM

NIAGARA FALLS TO QUEBEC.

BY WM. S. HUNTER, Jr.

Montreal:
PUBLISHED BY HUNTER & PICKUP.

PRINTED BY JOHN LOVELL, ST. NICHOLAS STREET.
1860.

198341

PREFACE.

THE following work is intended to supply what has long appeared a desideratum to the tourist who visits Niagara and the St. Lawrence,—a Panoramic or Picture Map of all the most celebrated and picturesque points along this noble river. The Author has, through a variety of difficulties and at great expense, finished the work which he contemplated; and however great may have been the task, the assurance and encouragement of many friends give him every reason to believe, that he will have no cause to regret the attempt of bringing before the public his Panoramic Guide from Niagara to Quebec.

As the country embraced in the range of his illustrated scenery has been fully explored and noticed by other travellers, the Author has not deemed it necessary to add long descriptions of the different towns and villages to his work. He trusts that his

Panorama itself will be found sufficient, mainly, for the object in view: viz., that of condensing much important matter within a very small space. In the selection of materials for description, he has, in addition to his own observations, availed himself of the various reliable sources of information to which he has had access. He has made free use of an excellent work, published in the form of a Hand-book, by R. W. S. Mackay, Esq.

To difference of taste, and a necessary limit to the extent of the work, must be assigned any apparent omissions, which those conversant with the scenery of the St. Lawrence may observe.

STANSTEAD, C. E., Oct. 25, 1856.

HUNTER'S PANORAMIC GUIDE.

APPROACH TO NIAGARA.

THE traveller in his first visit to this place is impressed with a sense of inexpressible amazement. His emotions are not unlike those of the votary of necromancy, who, when once within the magic circle, trembles under the influence of the enchanter, even before he confronts the wizard himself. A low sound, like the pealing of distant thunder, tells him plainly that he is approaching the wonder of wonders, THE FALLS OF NIAGARA!

HORSE SHOE FALL.

Who can forget his first view of this grand and stupendous spectacle? The roaring is so tremendous, that it would seem that if all the lions that ever have lived since the days of Daniel, could join their voices in one "Hullah's" chorus, they would produce but a whisper, in comparison to the deep diapason of this most majestic of all nature's pipes or organs.

HORSE SHOE FALL.

The wooden bridge which connects the mainland with Goat Island

HORSE SHOE FALLS—FROM CANADA SIDE.

HORSE SHOE FALLS—FROM THE AMERICAN SIDE.

is eagerly passed, and we explore the whole of this curious crag, which is rightly named, for it is found fantastically enough to suggest that goats only could find a comfortable footing. The sublimity of the scene increases at every step; but when we come upon the mighty Cataract, we gaze in speechless wonder. But words cannot describe the grandeur of this scene, nor the emotions which it excites; neither can the pencil, any more than the pen, do it justice. The silent and the still picture wants the motion and the sound of that stupendous rush of waters. It is impossible to paint the ever rising column of spray that spires upward from the foaming gulf below, or the prismatic glory that crowns it; for there indeed has God forever "set his bow" in the cloud, and cold must be the heart that in such a scene remembers not his covenant.

THE RAPIDS.

As neither descriptive language nor pictorial art can give an adequate conception of the magnitude of this wondrous Cataract, some notion may be suggested of the immense volume of water falling over the precipice, when it has been computed to be nearly 20,000,000 cubic feet per minute, in the Horse Shoe Fall alone; to say nothing of the Fall on the American side. The Horse Shoe Fall is 1900 feet across, and 158 feet in height; the American Fall is 908 feet wide, and 164 feet high. It is calculated that those Falls recede at the rate of a foot every year. It is here that the beautiful phenomenon of the rainbow is seen to such advantage.

TABLE ROCK.

This is truly a magnificent crag, — the projection at the top being immense, from which large masses are often falling. Many accidents have happened to tourists venturing too near the precipice. A small steamer, called "The Maid of the Mist," plies up and down the river, for two or three miles, and ventures even close under the Falls. Some travellers are also fond of dressing themselves in tarpaulin clothing, and going behind the projection of the impending

FROM NIAGARA FALLS TO QUEBEC.

TABLE ROCK—NIAGARA FALLS.

cliff, behind the mighty Fall; but the danger is, we consider, far too great for the mere sake of saying that we have been under Niagara. The Table Rock, however, exists now but in memory, for it suddenly fell some years ago. Had this accident occurred an hour or two earlier in the day, the Victoria Bridge, the Grand Trunk Railway, and all other Canadian undertakings thereunto pertaining, would be a dream of the future, and not a substantiality of the present; for a very short time previous to the disappearance of the slippery granite, there were standing upon it, viewing the Falls, the engineer of the Bridge, and several of his colleagues in the enterprises that have been mentioned.

ENTRANCE TO THE CAVE OF THE WINDS.

About three miles below the Falls is a frightfully wild spot, called the Whirlpool. The ravine is termed the Bloody Run, from a sanguinary engagement between two hostile Indian tribes. No human effort could possibly rescue the unfortunate individual who should happen to become entangled in the eddies of this pool.

It is supposed that there is a subterraneous current from this spot. Between it and the Falls there was a temporary suspension bridge; but it has been superseded by a stronger one for the Great Western Railway of Canada. Close to the Falls is a very fine hotel, situated on the Canadian side, from whence the two Falls may be seen to great advantage; although the choicest point of view we consider to be above the Falls altogether. Nothing can exceed the grandeur of the view here; and, to repeat a former remark, no art or description can fully realize the beauty and sublimity of the scene.

THE DEVIL'S HOLE

is a large triangular chasm in the bank of the river, three and a half miles below the Falls. The Bloody Run, as previously mentioned, falls into this chasm.

The following tale will, we think, be read with interest, in connection with Niagara.

THE HERMIT OF THE FALLS.

About twenty-five years since, in the glow of early summer, a young stranger of pleasing countenance and person made his appearance at Niagara. It was at first conjectured that he was an artist, a large portfolio, with books and musical instruments, being among his baggage. He was deeply impressed with the majesty and sublimity of the Cataract and the surrounding scenery, and expressed an intention to remain a week, that he might survey them at his leisure. But the fascination, which all minds of sensibility feel in the presence of that glorious work of the Creator, grew strongly upon him, and he was heard to say that six weeks were insufficient to become acquainted with its beauties. At the end of that period he was still unable to tear himself away, and desired to "build there a tabernacle," that he might indulge in his love of solitary musings, and admire at leisure the sublimity of nature. He applied for a spot on the Three Sisters' Island, on which to erect a cottage after his own model; one of the peculiarities of which was a drawbridge, to insure isolation. Circumstances forbidding compliance with this request, he took up his residence in an old house on Iris Island, which he rendered as comfortable as the state of the case would admit. Here he remained about eighteen months, when the intrusion of a family interrupted his habits of seclusion and meditation. He then quietly withdrew, and reared for himself a less commodious habitation near Prospect Point. When winter came, a cheerful fire of wood blazed upon the hearth, and he beguiled the long hours of evening by reading and music. It was strange to hear, in such a solitude, the long-drawn, thrilling notes of the viol, or the softest melody of the flute, gushing forth from that low-browed hut, or the guitar breathing out so lightly amid the rush and thunder of the never slumbering torrent. Though the world of letters was familiar to his mind, and the living world to his observation, for he had travelled widely, both in his native Europe and the East, he sought not association with mankind, to unfold or to increase his stores of knowledge. Those who had occasionally conversed with him, spoke with equal surprise and admiration of his colloquial powers, his command of language, and his fervid eloquence; but he seldom and sparingly admitted this intercourse, studiously avoiding society; though there seemed in his nature nothing of misanthropy or moroseness. On the contrary, he showed kindness to even the humblest animals. Birds instinctively learned this amiable trait in his character, and freely entered his dwelling, to receive from his hands crumbs or seeds.

But the absorbing delight of his solitary residence, was communion with Niagara. Here he might be seen at every hour of the day or night, a fervent worshipper. At the gray dawn he went to visit it in the vail of mist; at noon, he banqueted in the full splendor of its glory; beneath the soft tinting of the lunar bow he lingered, looking for the angel whose pencil had painted it; and, at solemn midnight, he knelt at the same shrine. Neither the storms of autumn, nor the piercing cold of winter, prevented his visits to the temple of his adoration. There was, at this time, an extension of the Serappin Bridge, by a single beam of timber, carried out ten feet over the fathomless abyss, where it hung tremulously, guarded only by a rude parapet. Along this beam he often passed and repassed, in the darkness of night. He even took pleasure in grasping it with his hands, and thus suspending himself over the awful gulf; so much had his morbid enthusiasm taught him to revel amid the terribly sublime. Among his favorite gratifications, was that of bathing, in which he indulged daily.

One bright but rather chilly day in the month of June, 1831, a man, employed about the ferry, saw him go into the water, and for a long time after observed his clothes to be still lying upon the bank. The poor hermit had taken his last bath. It was supposed that cramp might have been induced by the chill of the atmosphere or the water. Still the body was not found, the depth and force of the current below being exceedingly great. In the course of their search, they passed on to the Whirlpool. There, amid those boiling eddies, was the body, making fearful and rapid gyrations upon the face of the black waters. At some point of suction, it suddenly plunged and disappeared. Again emerging, it was fearful to see it leap half its length above the flood, then float motionless, as if exhausted, and, anon, spring upward, and seem to struggle like a maniac battling with a mortal foe. For days and nights this terrible scene was prolonged. It was not until the 21st of June, that, after many efforts, they were able to recover the body, and bear it to his desolate cottage. There they found his faithful dog, guarding the door. Heavily had the long period worn away, while he watched for his only friend, and wondered why he delayed his coming. He scrutinized the approaching group suspiciously, and would not willingly have given them admittance. A stifled wail at length showed his intuitive knowledge of the master, whom the work of death had effectually disguised from the eyes of men. On the pillow was his pet kitten, and in different parts of the room were his guitar, flute, violin, portfolio, and books, scattered, — the books open, as if recently used. It was a touching sight; the hermit mourned by his humble retainers, the poor animals that loved him, and ready to be laid by strange hands in a foreign grave.

The motives that led this singular and accomplished being, learned in the languages, in the arts and sciences, improved by extensive travel, and gifted with personal beauty and a feeling heart, to seclude himself, in the flower of youth, from human society, are still enveloped in mystery. All that is known was, that his name was Francis Abbot, that he was a native of England, where his father was a clergyman, and that he had received from thence ample remittances for his comfort. These facts had been previously ascertained, but no written papers were found in his cell to throw additional light upon the obscurity in which he had so effectually wrapped the history of his pilgrimage. The lovers of romance have, however, identified his history with that of the hero of several modern tales, in which, as a matter of course, it is asserted that * * *

NIAGARA CITY.

From the beautiful view here obtained of the Falls, this place was formerly called Bellevue. The village has mostly grown up since the time of the erection of the Suspension Bridge, at this point. The population now numbers about 1200, and is rapidly increasing. A grist mill has been erected near the Bridge, the water-wheel of which is placed beneath, requiring a shaft 280 feet long to communicate with the mill, on the top of the bank. The town contains many fine buildings; prominent among these is a very large Railroad Depot. Niagara City has grown so rapidly, and is still so much upon the increase, that a general description only can be applied to it for any length of time.

LEWISTON.

This village is situated at the head of navigation, on the Lower Niagara, and is a place of considerable importance. It lies three miles below the Devil's Hole, and seven miles below the Falls. Lewiston is a pleasant, well built village, but its commercial prospects have been very much injured by the construction of the Erie and Welland Canals.

THE SUSPENSION BRIDGE,

at this point, is one of the most stupendous works of the age. The span of this Bridge is one thousand and forty-five feet. It is carried over large towers of cut stone, and secured by anchors sunk firmly into the solid rock. It is supported by five cables upon each side. Each cable is composed of 250 strands of number ten wire, 1245 feet in length. The extreme capacity of the bridge is estimated at eight hundred and thirty-five tons. This bridge was erected in 1850, under the superintendence of E. W. Serrell, Esq., of Canada East, and is the property of a joint company of Canadians and Americans.

SUSPENSION BRIDGE.

QUEENSTON.

This is a small village, situated nearly opposite to Lewiston, and contains about 200 inhabitants. It is the Canadian termination of the Bridge, and is associated in history with the gallant defence made by the British, on the adjacent heights, in the war of 1812. The village is pleasantly situated, but it has suffered from the same causes that have retarded the growth of Lewiston.

QUEENSTON SUSPENSION BRIDGE.

Near this point the river becomes more tranquil, the shores appear less broken and wild, and the change in the scenery affords a pleasing transition from the sublime to the beautiful.

BROCK'S MONUMENT.

This Monument stands on the Heights of Queenston, from whence the village derived its name. The present structure occupies the site of the former one, which was blown up by some miscreant, on the 17th of April, 1840. The whole edifice is one hundred and eighty-five feet high. On the sub-base, which is forty feet square and thirty feet high, are placed four lions, facing north, south, east, and west; the base of the pedestal is twenty-one and a half feet square, and ten feet high; the pedestal itself is sixteen feet square, and ten feet high, surmounted with a heavy cornice, ornamented with lion heads and wreaths, in alto-relievo. In ascending from the top of the pedestal to the top of the base of the shaft, the form changes from square to round. The shaft is a fluted column of

RUIN OF THE OLD BROCK MONUMENT.

freestone, seventy-five feet high and ten feet in diameter; on which stands a Corinthian capital, ten feet high, on which is wrought, in relief, a statue of the Goddess of War. On this capital is the dome, nine feet high, which is reached by 250 spiral steps from the base, on the inside. On the top of the dome is placed a colossal statue of Gen. Brock.

FORT NIAGARA.

This Fort stands at the mouth of the Niagara River, on the American side. There are many interesting associations connected with this spot; as, during the earlier part of the past century, it was the scene of many severe conflicts between the Whites and the Indians, and subsequently between the English and the French. The names of the heroic La Salle, the courtly De Nouville, and the gallant Prideaux, will long retain a place in the history of this country. The village adjacent to the Fort is called Youngstown, in honor of its founder, the late John Young, Esq.

FORT NIAGARA.

NIAGARA.

This is one of the oldest towns in Upper Canada, and was formerly the capital of the Province. It is situated where the old town of Newark stood, and is opposite to Youngstown. It faces the river on one side, and Lake Ontario on the other. The trade of this place has been diverted to St. Catherine's, since the completion of the Welland Canal; and the other towns upon the Niagara River have suffered in common, from the same cause.

FORT MASSASAUGA.

TORONTO,

the Capital City in Upper Canada, is situated on an arm of Lake Ontario, thirty-six miles from the mouth of Niagara River. This city was formerly called Little York. The first survey was made in 1793. Toronto Bay is a beautiful inlet, separated from the main body of Lake Ontario, except at its entrance, by a long, narrow, sandy beach. The south-western extremity is called Gibraltar Point. The population, in 1817, was 1200; but, at the present time, it amounts to about 60,000. With a similar progress for a few years to come, the population of this city will be second to none in British America. Among the principal buildings of Toronto, are a University and a Cathedral. One of the ecclesiastical edifices deserves especial notice,—the Church of The Holy Trinity; a handsome structure, erected by a donation of five thousand pounds from some liberal person from England, on condition that the whole of the seats should be free. The Elgin Association, for improving the moral and religious condition of the colored population, is among the most useful institutions of the place. That stupendous undertaking, the Grand Trunk Railway of Canada, passes through Toronto, and promises a splendid future, not only for this city, but for every other city in the country; for the benefits to be derived from it are incalculable. Nature has bestowed fine rivers and vast lakes, which have already been made fully subservient to commerce; but how wonderfully will commerce be advanced by the linking of these lakes and rivers by means of railways. Thus will be constituted one great unbroken medium of speedy communication from the far West of America to the shores of the Atlantic.*

LAKE ONTARIO.

This wonderful sheet of fresh water is 235 feet above the level of the sea, 100 fathoms deep, 200 miles long, and 60 miles wide; therefore, in crossing it, one necessarily loses sight of land altogether. Nothing can be more delightful than sailing on its magnificent

---

* For further particulars respecting this city, see McKay's Stranger's Guide.

HUNTER'S PANORAMIC GUIDE

A PORTION OF THE CITY OF TORONTO.

bosom, on a beautiful summer night; but when the storm arises, its placid character is gone, and we are made to feel that it is a sea in power, and may be so in swift destructiveness; for in these land-locked basins shipwrecks often occur, not merely of the frail barks of commerce, but even of the stout-built man of war, should she, when caught in one of the fierce gales which so suddenly sweep the lake, be unable to run for her harbor. The harbor of British armed vessels, in the waters of this lake, is Kingston.

LAKE ONTARIO STEAMER.

LAKE ONTARIO FROM NIAGARA RIVER.

PORT HOPE

is situated **sixty-five** miles from Toronto. A small stream, which here falls into the Lake, has formed a valley, in which the town is located. The harbor formed at the mouth of this stream is shallow, but safe and commodious. Port Hope is a very pretty town; on the western side, the hills rise gradually one above another. The highest summit, which is called "Fort Orton," affords a fine prospect, and overlooks the country for a great distance around. The village is incorporated, and contains about 2200 inhabitants.

COBOURG

lies seven miles below Port Hope, and contains 4000 inhabitants. The town contains seven churches, two banks, three grist mills, two foundries, and the largest cloth factory in the province. It is also the seat of Victoria College and a Theological Institute. Midway between Port Hope and Cobourg is "Duck Island," on which a lighthouse is maintained by the government.

KINGSTON.

This place was called by the Indians, "*Cataraequi.*" A settlement was begun by the French, under De Courcelles, as early as 1672. The Fort, which was finished the next year, was called Fort Frontenac, in honor of the French count of that name. This Fort was alternately in the possession of the French and the Indians, until it was destroyed by the expedition under Col. Bradstreet, in 1758. In 1762, the place fell into the hands of the English, from whom it received its present name. Kingston is one of the most important military posts in Canada. It is one hundred and ten miles from Cobourg, and contains about 11,000 inhabitants.

KINGSTON.

[Before proceeding down the St. Lawrence, we will retrace our steps, and briefly notice the places on the American side of Lake Ontario.]

CHARLOTTESVILLE

is situated at the mouth of the Gennesee River, and is the port of entry for Rochester. It is seventy-five miles from the mouth of the Niagara. The Gennesee is navigable by steamers to Carthage, five miles from its mouth. At Carthage, passengers can take omnibuses to Rochester, two miles distant.

OSWEGO

is the next port, after passing Charlottesville. It is a beautiful and flourishing town, and contains a population of about 15,000. It is

FROM NIAGARA FALLS TO QUEBEC.

CITY OF KINGSTON, C. W.

the commercial centre of a fertile and wealthy part of the country, and is the terminus of a railroad and a canal, connecting it with Syracuse and the New York Central Railway. The history of this place is associated with many hard battles, fought during the time of the Indian and the French wars.

CAPE ST. VINCENT RAILROAD DEPOT.

SACKETT'S HARBOR.

This place is situated about forty-five miles from Oswego, and twenty miles from the St. Lawrence. It lies upon the north-eastern shore of Lake Ontario, and derives its name from Mr. Sackett, of Jamaica, L. I., who purchased and took possession of it in 1799. It is admirably fitted, from its position, for a naval station, and is now the seat of a military post, called "Madison Barracks."

THE THOUSAND ISLANDS

are amongst the wonders of the St. Lawrence; situated about six miles below Kingston. There are, in fact, no less than 1800 of these "emerald gems in the ring of the wave," of all sizes, from the islet

FORT HENRY — MARTELLO TOWER
CEDAR ISLAND.

LIGHTHOUSE ON ONE OF THE
THOUSAND ISLANDS.

a few yards square, to miles in length. It is a famous spot for sporting; myriads of wild fowls of all descriptions may here be found; and angling is rather fatiguing than otherwise, from the great quantity and size of the fish. These islands, too, have been the scene of most exciting romance. From their great number, and the labyrinth-like channels among them, they afforded an admirable retreat for the insurgents in the last Canadian insurrection, and for the American sympathizers with them; who, under the questionable name of "patriots," sought only to embarrass the British Government. Among these was one man, who, from his daring and ability,

VIEWS AMONG THE THOUSAND ISLANDS.

became an object of anxious pursuit to the Canadian authorities; and he found a safe asylum in these watery intricacies, through the devotedness and courage of his daughter, whose inimitable management of her canoe was such, that through hosts of pursuers she baffled their efforts at capture, while she supplied him with provisions in these solitary retreats, rowing him from one place of concealment to another, under shadow of the night. But, in truth, all the islands, which are so numerously studded through the whole chain of those magnificent Lakes, abound with materials for romance and poetry. For instance, in the Manitoulin Islands, in Lake Huron, the Indians believe that the *Manitou*, that is, the *Great Spirit* (and hence the name of the islands) has forbidden his children to seek for gold; and they tell you that a certain point, where it is reported to exist in large quantities, has never been visited by the disobedient Indian without his canoe being overwhelmed in a tempest.

CLAYTON.

This village is situated on the American side, opposite to the "Thousand Islands," and is of considerable importance as a lumber station. Square timber and staves are here made up into large rafts, and floated down the St. Lawrence to Montreal and Quebec. These rafts are often very large; and as they require a great number of men to navigate them, the huts erected for their shelter give them, as they pass down the river, the appearance of small villages. Many of the steamers and other craft that navigate Lake Ontario are built here.

ALEXANDRIA BAY

is the next port, after leaving Clayton. It is built upon a massive pile of rocks, and its situation is romantic and highly picturesque. It is a place of resort for sportsmen. Some two or three miles below the village, is a position from whence one hundred islands can be seen at one view.

BROCKVILLE.

This village was named in honor of General Brock, who fell on Queenston Heights, in the war of 1812. It is situated on the Canadian side of the St. Lawrence, and is one of the pleasantest villages in the province. It is situated at the foot of the Thousand Islands, on an elevation of land which rises from the river in a succession of ridges. The town was laid out in 1802, and is now a place of considerable importance. The present population is about 2500.

OGDENSBURGH.

In the year 1748, the Abbé Francois Piquet, who was afterwards styled the "Apostle of the Iroquois," was sent to establish a mission at this place, as many of the Indians of that tribe had manifested a desire of embracing Christianity. A settlement was began in connection with this mission, and a fort, called "La Presentation," was built at the mouth of the Oswegatchie, on the west side. The remains of the walls of this Fort are still to be seen. In October, 1749, it was attacked by a band of Indians from the Mohawks, who, although bravely repulsed, succeeded in destroying the pallisades of the fort, and two of the vessels belonging to the colony. The Abbé Piquet retired from the settlement soon after the defeat of Montcalm, and finally returned to France, where he died in 1781.

In describing the situation of the ground on the east side of the river, opposite to his fort, the Abbé, with his accustomed discrimination, remarked: "A beautiful town could hereafter be built here." This prediction has been fully verified; and the village of Ogdensburgh now occupies this site. It is a flourishing town. It has increased rapidly within the few past years, and will doubtless become a large manufacturing place. The Northern Railroad, which runs to Lake Champlain, a distance of one hundred and eighteen miles, and which connects at Rouse's Point with the railroads to Boston and Montreal, has its terminus here.

PRESCOTT

is situated on the Canada side of the St. Lawrence, opposite Ogdensburgh, and contains about 3000 inhabitants. Previous to the opening of the Rideau Canal between Kingston and Ottawa City (formerly Bytown), Prescott was a place of importance in the carrying trade between Kingston and Montreal; but since that event its growth has been checked. Matters have, however, again changed, and for Prescott there are prospects of brighter days to come. Through the influence, and energy, and untiring perseverance of Robert Bell, Esq., of Ottawa City, a railroad has been built, under almost insurmountable obstacles, which extends from Ottawa City to Prescott, and there connects the Ottawa River with the St. Lawrence. The enterprise has, thus far, more than realized the most sanguine hopes of its projector. About a mile below the town of Prescott, at a place called "Windmill Point," are the ruins of an old stone windmill, in which, in 1837, the "Patriots," under Von Shultz, a Polish exile, established themselves, but from which they were driven with severe loss. About five miles below Prescott is Chimney Island, on which the remains of an old French fortification are to be seen. The first rapid of the St. Lawrence, is at this island.

WINDMILL POINT.

The next town on the American side is Waddington; and in the river, over against it, is Ogden Island. On the Canada side is Morrisburg, formerly called West Williamsburg. It is called the Port of Morristown, and contains about two hundred inhabitants.

GALLOPS RAPIDS.

CHRYSELER'S FARM.

A short distance below Morristown, on the Canada side, is Chryseler's Farm, where, in 1813, a battle was fought between the English and the Americans. The Americans were commanded by Gen. Wilkinson, and were at that time descending the river to attack Montreal. The attempt was afterwards abandoned. Thirty miles below Ogdensburgh is Louisville, from whence stages run to Massena Springs, distant seven miles.

LONG SAULT.

This is a continuous rapid of nine miles, divided in the centre by an island. The usual passage for steamers is on the south side. The channel on the north side was formerly considered unsafe and dangerous; but examinations have been made, and it is now descended with safety. The passage in the southern channel is very narrow, and such is the velocity of the current that a raft, it is said, will drift the nine miles in forty minutes.

DESCENT OF THE RAPIDS.

This is the most exciting part of the whole passage of the St. Lawrence. The rapids of the "Long Sault" rush along at the rate of something like twenty miles an hour. When the vessel enters within their influence the steam is shut off and she is carried

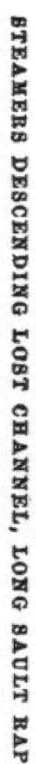

STEAMERS DESCENDING LOST CHANNEL, LONG SAULT RAPIDS

HUNTER'S PANORAMIC GUIDE

BATISTE, AN INDIAN PILOT, STEERING A STEAMER DOWN THE RAPIDS OF THE ST. LAWRENCE.

onwards by the force of the stream alone. The surging waters present all the angry appearance of the ocean in a storm; the noble boat strains and labors: but, unlike the ordinary pitching and tossing at sea, this going down hill by water produces a highly novel sensation, and is, in fact, a service of some danger, the imminence of which is enhanced to the imagination by the tremendous roar of the headlong, boiling current. Great nerve, and force, and precision are here required in piloting, so as to keep the vessel's head straight with the course of the rapid; for if she diverged in the least, presenting her side to the current, or "broached to," as the nautical phrase is, she would be instantly capsized and submerged. Hence the necessity for enormous power over her rudder; and for this purpose the mode of steering affords great facility, for the wheel that governs the rudder is placed ahead, and by means of chain and pulley sways it. But in descending the rapids a tiller is placed astern to the rudder itself, so that the tiller can be manned as well as the wheel. Some idea may be entertained of the peril of descending a rapid, when it requires four men at the wheel and two at the tiller to ensure safe steering. Here is the region of the daring raftsmen, at whose hands are demanded infinite courage and skill; and, despite of both, loss of life frequently occurs.

LONG SAULT RAPIDS.

VIEW IN THE LONG SAULT.

RAFT DESCENDING THE RAPIDS.

HUNTER'S PANORAMIC GUIDE

ST. LAWRENCE CANALS.

	Miles.	Locks.	L. Ft.
Gallops Canal,	2	2	8.
Point Iroquois Canal,	3	1	6.
Rapid Platt Canal,	4	2	11.6
Farren's Point Canal	¾	1	4.
Cornwall Canal, Long Sault,	11½	7	48.
Beauharnois Canal, Coteau,			
Cedars, Split Rock, Cascade Rapids,	11¼	9	82.6
La Chine Canal, La Chine Rapids,	8½	5	44.9
Fall on portions of the St. Lawrence between canals from Lake Ontario to Montreal,			17.
From Montreal to tide water at Three Rivers,			12.9
	41	27	234.½

The St. Lawrence canal was designed for paddle steamers, but from the magnitude of the rapids and their regular inclination the aid of the locks is not required in descending the river. Large steamers, drawing seven feet water, with passengers and the mails, leave the foot of Lake Ontario in the morning, and reach the wharves at Montreal by daylight, without passing through a single

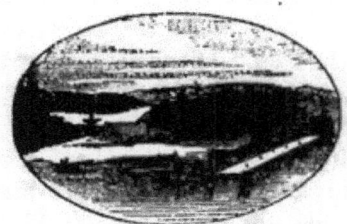
ENTRANCE TO CORNWALL CANAL.

DICKINSON'S LANDING.

lock. At some of the rapids there are obstacles preventing the descent of deeply laden craft; but the government are about to give the main channel in all the rapids a depth of ten feet water, when the whole descending trade by steam will keep the river, leaving the canals to the ascending craft.

CORNWALL.

This is a pleasant town, situated at the foot of the Long Sault, on the Canada side. Here vessels are passed up the river by the Cornwall canal, and come out into the river about twelve miles above. The boundary line between the United States and Canada passes near this village, and the course of the St. Lawrence is hereafter within Her Majesty's dominions.

ST. REGIS

is an old Indian village, and lies a little below Cornwall, on the opposite side of the river. It contains a Catholic church, which was built about the year 1700. While the building was in progress, the Indians were told by their priest that a bell was indispensable in their house of worship, and they were ordered to collect furs sufficient to purchase one. The furs were collected, the money was sent to France, and the bell was bought and shipped for Canada; but the vessel which contained it was captured by an English cruiser, and taken into Salem, Massachusetts. The bell was afterwards purchased for the church at Deerfield. The priest of St. Regis, having heard of its destination, excited the Indians to a general crusade for its recovery. They joined the expedition fitted out by the governor against the New England colonists, and proceeded through the then long, trackless wilderness, to Deerfield, which they attacked in the night. The inhabitants, unsuspicious of danger, were aroused from sleep only to meet the tomahawk and scalping-knife of the savages. Forty-seven were killed, and one hundred and twelve taken captive; among whom were Mr. Williams, the pastor, and his family. Mrs. Williams being at the time feeble, and not able to travel with her husband and family, was killed by the Indians. Mr. Williams and a part of his surviving family afterwards returned to Deerfield, but the others remained with the Indians, and became connected with the tribe. The Rev. Eleazar Williams, one of the supposed descendants from this family,

ST. REGIS INDIANS.

has been mysteriously identified with the lost Dauphin of France. The Indians, after having completed their work of destruction, fastened the bell to a long pole, and carried it upon their shoulders a distance of nearly one hundred and fifty miles, to the place where Burlington now stands; they buried it there, and in the following spring removed it to the church at St. Regis, where it now hangs.

LAKE ST. FRANCIS

This is the name of that expansion of the St. Lawrence which begins near Cornwall and St. Regis, and extends to Coteau du Lac, a distance of forty miles. The surface of this lake is interspersed with a great number of small islands. The village of Lancaster is situated on the northern side, about midway of this lake.

COTEAU DU LAC

is a small village, situated at the foot of Lake St. Francis. The name, as well as the style of the buildings, denotes its French origin. Just below the village are the Coteau Rapids.

CEDARS.

This village presents the same marks of French origin as Coteau du Lac. In the expedition of Gen. Amherst, a detachment of three hundred men, that were sent to attack Montreal, were lost in the rapids near this place. The passage through these rapids is very exciting. There is a peculiar motion of the vessel, which in descending seems like settling down, as she glides from one ledge to another. In passing the rapids of the Split Rock, a person unacquainted with the navigation of these rapids will almost involuntarily hold his breath until this ledge of rocks, which is distinctly seen from the deck of the steamer, is passed. At one time the vessel seems to be running directly upon it, and you feel

CEDAR RAPIDS.

HUNTER'S PANORAMIC GUIDE

certain that she will strike; but a skilful hand is at the helm, and in an instant more it is passed in safety.

BEAUHARNOIS

is a small village at the foot of the Cascades, on the south bank of the river. Here vessels enter the Beauharnois canal, and pass around the rapids of the Cascades, Cedars, and Coteau, into lake St. Francis, a distance of fourteen miles. On the north bank, a branch of the Ottawa enters into the St. Lawrence. The river again widens into a lake called the St. Louis. From this place a view is had of Montreal Mountain, nearly thirty miles distant. In this lake is Nun's Island, which is beautifully cultivated, and belongs to the Gray Nunnery, at Montreal. There

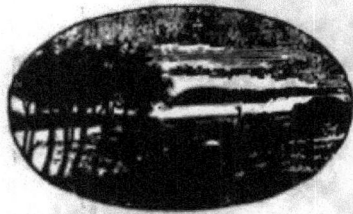

CASCADES FROM ENTRANCE TO BEAUHARNOIS CANAL.

NUN'S ISLAND.

are many islands in the vicinity of Montreal belonging to the different nunneries, and from which they derive large revenues.

LA CHINE.

This village is nine miles from Montreal, with which it is connected by railroad. The La Chine Rapids begin just below the town. The current is here so swift and wild that to avoid it a canal has been cut around these rapids. This canal is a stupendous work, and reflects much credit upon the energy and enterprise of the people of Montreal.

CAUGHNAWAGA.

This is an Indian village lying on the south bank of the river, near the entrance of the La Chine Rapids. It derived its name from the Indians that had been converted by the Jesuits, who were called "*Caughnawagas*," or "praying Indians." This was probably a misnomer, for they were distinguished for their predatory incursions upon their neighbors in the New England provinces. The bell that now hangs in their church was the "proceeds" of one of these excursions. The village of La Prairie is some seven miles below Caughnawaga.

CAUGHNAWAGA VILLAGE.

MONTREAL,

the largest and most populous city in British North America, is situated upon the island of the same name, in latitude 45 deg. 31 min. north, and longitude 63 deg. 34 min. west, from Greenwich. Including the suburbs, it covers an area of about one thousand and twenty acres, of which the ground within the old fortification does not comprise much more than one tenth part.

Jacques Cartier, the first European who explored this country, ascended the St. Lawrence in 1535, and found, at this place, a large Indian village, called Hochelaga. It was on the site of this village that M. de Maissoneuve, in 1642, founded the city, which for a long time bore the name of "*Ville Marie*," having been dedicated to the Virgin Mary as its patroness and protector. Although this place advanced rapidly into prosperity and importance, its growth was not unattended with those savage cruelties so fatally incident to the early settlements on this continent. In the summer of 1668, a party of Iroquois Indians, the inveterate enemies of the French, stealthily landed their canoes upon the island, and cruelly massacred men, women, and children, to the number of more than ten thousand. Only three of the confederate Indians, it is said, were lost in this scene of misery and desolation. It was soon peopled again,

however, and continued for a long time the head-quarters of the French forces in Canada. After the peace, in 1763, it was surrendered to the English, who held it until 1775, when it was taken by the Americans under Gen. Montgomery. The Americans were not able to hold the place long, and soon surrendered it back to the English.

Montreal is laid out in the form of a parallelogram. The streets, which are two hundred in number, intersect each other at right angles. *Notre Dame Street*, which is the principal street for retail business, is over three quarters of a mile in length. *Great St. James Street* is elegant and spacious, and is occupied principally by the banks and insurance companies. *St. Paul Street* is more than three quarters of a mile long; the west end of it, and the streets which intersect it, being mostly taken up with wholesale warehouses. *Water Street, Commissioners Street,* and *Common Street,* face the St. Lawrence, the entire length of the city, and exhibit a splendid front of cut stone warehouses, which has a very imposing effect. *McGill Street* extends northward from the river to the Haymarket Square. It is a wide and pleasant street, and a large retail business is carried on in it. *St. Antoine Street, Mountain Street, West Dorchester Street, Sherbrooke Street,* and the streets and squares on *Beaver Hill,* contain many beautiful private residences and villas, and are considered the most fashionable part of the city.

No one who visits this city should omit a ride around the Mountain. This is over a fine macadamized road, and passes many delightful residences. From the Mountain a nobler view is scarcely to be seen in the world. In the far distance tower the evergreen hills of Vermont; a magnificent plain, stretching miles and miles on either hand, studded with cultivated farms; the splendid River St. Lawrence, two miles wide, intervening, crossed by the stupendous tubular railway Victoria Bridge, now being constructed here.*
In the whole history of engineering there is nothing like so truly gigantic an undertaking. When finished it will be not only among the greatest wonders of America, but of the world. It is the creation of the same genius which has already spanned the Menai Straits with that unequalled fabric which so amazes all beholders, as com-

* See p. 48.

bining the massive solidity of the pyramids with the aerial tracery of Saracenic architecture. The Britania tubular suspension bridge, as is well known, is so called from the Britania Rock, which stands in the centre of the Menai Strait. On this rock is built a tower two hundred feet above high water, and on it rest two lines of tubes, or hollow girders, strong enough to bear their weight and laden railway trains in addition, the ends reposing on the abutment on either shore, each tube being more than a quarter of a mile in length; the interior height thirty feet at the Britania Tower diminishing to twenty-three at the abutments. Yet these dimensions, immense as they are, dwarf into Lilliputian insignificance beside the Titanic proportions of the Victoria Bridge.

This structure will contain twenty-five arches, of the uniform span of two hundred and forty-two feet. The tube is iron, the rest solid masonry, including the piers jutting into the river on either side, each about half a mile long; the centre arch will be sixty feet from the water level to the floor of the tube, which is twenty-five feet high and eighteen feet wide. It is calculated that each buttress will have to bear the pressure of seventy thousand tons of ice, when the winter breaks up and the large ice-fields come sweeping down the St. Lawrence. Hence the necessity for such buttresses being peculiarly designed for the purpose of effecting the disruption of those formidable assailants, and hence the necessity for the personal supervision of the work by Mr. Stephenson himself. How insignificant seem many of the most celebrated engineering works of antiquity beside an achievement of this nature. What a pigmy would not the Colossus of Rhodes be, under whose legs a ship of that period (290 B. C.) could pass in full sail, were he placed beneath the centre arch of Stephenson's much more colossal road, the Victoria Bridge! In connection with this bridge,

MONTREAL AND VICTORIA BRIDGE.

The GRAND TRUNK RAILWAY of Canada is, we consider, entitled to notice, on account both of its magnitude and importance. Includ-

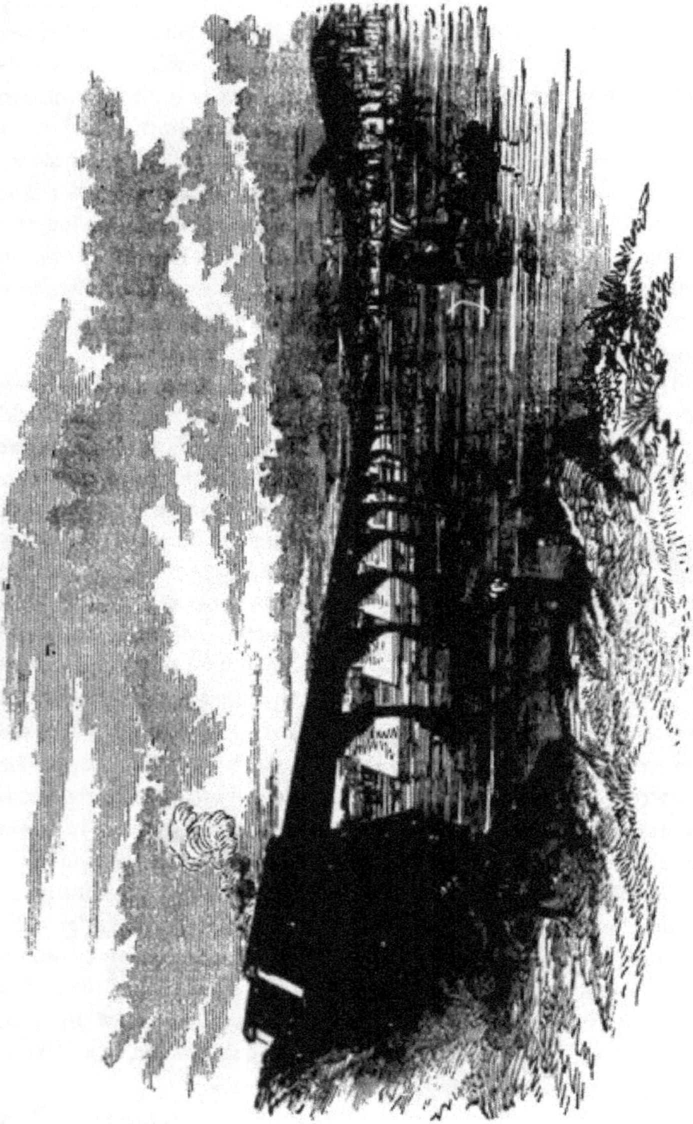

VICTORIA BRIDGE—MONTREAL.

ing the Atlantic and St. Lawrence portion, of which it has lately obtained a lease, its length when completed will be 1112 miles. Upwards of 800 miles is now opened and in operation; namely, from Portland to Montreal, 292 miles, and 100 miles from Richmond Junction to Point Levi, opposite Quebec; from Point Levi to St. Thomas, 40 miles; from Montreal to Toronto, C. W., 333 miles. Trains now run in summer from Quebec to Boston, via Portland (421 miles), in fifteen hours. Toronto can now be reached from Montreal in twelve or thirteen hours.

The population on and within fifteen miles of the Grand Trunk Railway is about a million and a half, and is rapidly increasing. Making the most ample allowance for competition by water, the average contribution of each resident within its influence (found to amount in the case of the United States railroads to $2.50 per annum), can fairly be estimated for the Grand Trunk at $1.60 for each individual, which will give an annual income, from this source alone, of $2,400,000. Canadians are justly proud of this gigantic railway.

Montreal being at the head of ship navigation, her local advantages for the purposes of trade are numerous. The completion of

LIVERPOOL AND MONTREAL SCREW STEAMER.

the Grand Trunk Railroad and the ocean line of steamers, recently established between Montreal and Liverpool, has added greatly to its commercial importance. From whatever side the city is approached, the scene is one of much interest. If from the St. Lawrence, the splendid towers of the cathedral, the tall spires of Christ Church, St. Patrick's Church, and several others, the elegant front of the Bonsecours Market, and the long ranges of cut stone buildings which front the river, form at once a "*tout ensemble*" which is perhaps unequalled in any other American city. And, although the prospects from the land side are not quite so imposing, they are all agreeable; and that from Côte des Neiges road (which crosses the spur of the mountain that overlooks the city), is, taken altogether, one of the finest in this part of the world.

The population of the city is about 65,000, and the number of inhabited houses about 8500. It is divided into nine wards, and is municipally governed by a mayor, aldermen, and council, elected by householders who pay an annual rent of $45 or upwards, or persons who own real estate producing half that amount of rent annually.

PLACES OF INTEREST TO THE TRAVELLER.

The new Court House, on Notre Dame street, nearly opposite Nelson's Monument. It is built of cut stone, in the Grecian Ionic style. Ground plan, three hundred by one hundred and twenty-five feet; height, seventy-six feet.

The new Post Office, Great St. James street, is a beautiful cut stone building of solid masonry, and reflects much credit upon its architect, John Wells, Esq.

The Merchants' Exchange, St. Sacrament street, in which edifice are several lines of telegraph offices, insurance offices, reading-room, &c.

The Mechanics' Institute is one of the finest buildings in the city, built in the Italian style. The principal lecture-room is sixty by eighty feet, with a height of eighteen feet, tastefully finished. One block from the Ottawa Hotel.

The Mercantile Library Association occupy for the present the Odd Fellows' Hall, opposite the Mechanics' Institute, but are about building an edifice which will do credit to the merchants' clerks in the city.

The Bank of Montreal is an elegant cut stone building of the Corinthian order, and reflects the highest credit upon the liberality of the managers of that institution. It is situated on the west side of the Place d'Armes.

The City Bank, on the northeast side of the Bank of Montreal, is built in the Grecian style of architecture, and of cut stone. A splendid building.

La Banque du Peuple, on the southwest side of the Bank of Montreal, is worthy of note, and is also built of cut stone.

The Bank of British North America adjoins the Post Office, and is no less an object of pride. Like most of the public buildings, it is of cut stone, and built in the Grecian style of architecture.

The Bonsecours Market, on St. Paul and Water streets, is a magnificent building in the Grecian and Doric style, erected at a cost of about three hundred thousand dollars. It has a front of three stories on Water street, and two on St. Paul street. The upper part of the building is occupied by the various offices of the city. The City Council room is fitted up in the most elegant style. In the east wing of the building is a large hall, or concert room, capable of seating four thousand persons.

The St. Ann's Market, Foundling street, although not built in the style of the Bonsecours, is still a building that speaks well for the spirit which governs the city in the erection of its public buildings.

The Gray Nunnery, on Foundling street, designed for the care of foundlings and the infirm.

The Hotel Dieu Nunnery, on St. Joseph and St. Paul streets, designed for sick and diseased persons of all denominations and classes.

The Academy of the Sisters of the Congregational Nunnery is a place well worthy of a visit by the traveller.

Maria Villa Academy. — This institution is beautifully situated about three miles from the city, and was formerly the residence of the governor-general, Lord Elgin. It is better known by the name of "Monkland."

The French Protestant Mission Institute is situated nine miles from the city. It contains over a hundred pupils, under Mr. Roux's direction.

McGill College. — This is an institution of very high repute. It was founded by the Hon. James McGill, who bequeathed a valuable estate and £10,000 for its endowment. The buildings for faculty of arts are delightfully situated at the base of the Mountain, and command an extensive view of the city and surrounding country.

The New City Water Works. Among the many enterprises, there are none which promise more general and useful advantages to the city, than the new works for supplying it with water. One of the greatest blessings is health, and nothing is more conducive to this than good pure water. This has now been secured by the erection of those works, which tap the St. Lawrence at the La Chine Rapids, some six miles above the city. These works will cost the city $1,000,000. The reservoirs are 200 feet above the level of the river, and contain twenty millions of gallons.

Nelson's Monument, at Jacques Cartier Square, is an object of interest. It was erected in 1801, and is consequently somewhat dilapidated now.

The Wharves of this city are unsurpassed by any on the American continent. No traveller should fail of visiting this portion of the city, as the wide stone walls along the parapet, for a distance of over a mile, and the refreshing breeze from the river, render it delightful in the extreme.

The La Chine Canal is among the public works particularly worthy of note, and of which the city may well feel proud.

The Victoria Bridge, now in progress, to cross the St. Lawrence, will be, when completed, the most stupendous structure in America. It will immensely advance the business prospects of Montreal, and will cost over $7,500,000.

Mount Royal Cemetery is situated on the east side of the Mountain, and about two miles from the city. It is much visited by strangers.

The Champ-de-Mars is a favorite promenade for citizens and strangers, being the general parade and review grounds of the military.

The Place d'Armes is a handsome square, opposite the French Cathedral, surrounded by a neat iron railing, and tastefully laid out and planted with shade trees. In the centre of the square is a fountain.

The French Parish Church is situated in Place d'Armes, and forms one of the most prominent attractions to strangers. The corner stone of this church was laid in 1824, and it was opened for worship in 1829. It contains 1244 pews, and will seat over

8000 persons. The towers of the church are 290 feet in height. In the northeast tower is a chime of bells, while the northwest contains the monster bell, the largest in America, weighing 24,000 lbs. This tower is always open to the public, by payment of a small fee; from the top is presented a panoramic view of the Island of Montreal, and well repays the fatigue of the ascent.

The St. Patrick's Church, situated on Lagauchetiere street.

St. James or *Bishop's Church*, Dennis street: a splendid building.

The Bonsecours Church, St. Paul street: the oldest church in the city.

The Bishop's Cathedral, together with his residence, are erected on the site of the old Roman Catholic Cemetery, St. Antoine suburbs.

Christ Church Cathedral (Protestant), on Notre Dame street, is a very fine building, capable of accommodating about two thousand persons, and is open daily for service throughout the year at 11 o'clock, A. M. On Sundays there are three services: viz., at half-past ten, A. M., at half-past one, P. M. (military service), and at three, P. M. The magnificent organ in this church was built in England, at a cost of £1600 sterling, and is the second largest in America.

The following are the most prominent of the remaining Protestant Churches in the city: viz., Trinity Church, St. Paul street; St. George's Church, St. Joseph street; St. Stephen's Church, Dalhousie street, Griffintown; St. Luke's Church, Quebec suburbs; St. Thomas' Church, Quebec suburbs; United Presbyterian Church, Lagauchetiere street; American Presbyterian Church, Great St. James street; St. Andrew's Church, Beaver Hall; St. Paul's Church, Helen street; Free Church, Coti street; Old Scotch Kirk, St. Gabriel street; Zion Church, Radegonde street; Lutheran Church (German), Gosford street; Wesleyan Church, Great St. James street; Baptist Church, Helen street; Unitarian Church, Beaver Hall; French Evangelical Church, Dorchester street.

HOTELS.

Montreal was formerly deficient in Hotels, but this defect has been remedied, and the city now abounds in fine ones, where every comfort can be found, and where visitors are well accommodated; amongst which are the Ottawa Hotel * and the St. Lawrence House, Great St. James street, the Montreal House, Custom House square, and the Donegana Hotel, Notre Dame street.

The traveller who is desirous of spending an hour in perusing the popular literature of the day, or matters of a more serious nature, will find an ample assortment of either at the stores of B. Dawson, George Sparkes, and E. Pickup.

As a description of all the points of interest connected with the city of Montreal would of itself fill a volume, and altogether transcend the limits of the present work, we have endeavored to present merely a brief outline or bird's-eye view, which, imperfect soever it may appear, may, as we would hope, be of service to the traveller in his first visit to this place.

In proceeding down the St. Lawrence, we pass the island of St. Helen, which lies opposite the lower part of the city of Montreal. The upper end of this island is covered with a fine grove of forest trees. The lower end is strongly fortified, and commands the passage of the river. A small rapid, called St. Mary's, is just below this island.

LONGUEUIL

is a small village on the south bank of the river, three miles below Montreal. It is important only as being the present terminus of the St. Lawrence and Atlantic Railroad.

WILLIAM HENRY,

or Sorel, is situated at the junction of the Richelieu, the outlet of Lake Champlain with the St. Lawrence. It is forty-five miles below Montreal, and is the first stopping-place for steamers on their way to Quebec. The town is laid out in the form of a quadrangle, and contains a number of good buildings, the principal of which

---

* While the other first-class houses in Montreal afford, as we believe, every accommodation and are well sustained, we consider ourselves justified in recommending this hotel particularly to the notice of visitors. Mr. Browning, the present proprietor, is distinguished for his attention to the comfort of his guests, and he spares no pains in "posting" them in all the interesting sights about the city and its vicinity. The publisher of this work feels it a duty to the public to speak in the highest terms of this establishment.

FROM NIAGARA FALLS TO QUEBEC.

are the Roman Catholic and the English churches. The population is about 8000.

LAKE ST. PETER'S

is an expansion of the St. Lawrence, beginning about five miles below Sorel, and extending in length twenty-five miles; its greatest

WRECK OF A RAFT ON LAKE ST. PETER'S.

breadth is nine miles. It is quite shallow, except in a narrow channel, which is now navigable for vessels of six hundred tons, and is in course of being improved, so as to admit vessels of one thousand tons ascending to Montreal. There are several islands at its western extremity. Port St. Francis is a small village, situated on the south shore of Lake St. Peter's, eighty-two miles below Montreal. It is a place of but little importance.

THREE RIVERS

is situated at the confluence of the rivers St. Maurice and St. Lawrence, ninety miles below Montreal, and the same distance above Quebec. It is one of the oldest settled towns in Canada, having been founded in 1618. It is well laid out, and contains many good buildings,

ROMAN CATHOLIC PARISH CHURCH.

NUNS.

among which are the court house, the jail, the Roman Catholic church, the Ursuline convent, and the English and Wesleyan churches. The population of Three Rivers is about 5500.

BATISCAN

is situated on the north shore of the river, one hundred and seventeen miles below Montreal. It is the last place at which the steamers stop before reaching Quebec. It is a place of little importance.

In passing down the St. Lawrence from Montreal, the country upon its banks presents a sameness in its general scenery, until we approach the vicinity of Quebec. The villages and hamlets are decidedly *French* in character, and are generally made up of small buildings, the better class of which are painted white or whitewashed, with red roofs. Prominent in the distance appear the tile-covered

CANADIAN HABITANS.

spires of the Catholic churches, which are all constructed in that unique style of architecture so peculiar to that church.

CANADIAN FARMHOUSE.

The rafts of timber afford a highly interesting feature on the

CANADIAN PRIEST.   CANADIAN PEASANT.

river as the traveller passes along. On each a shed is built for the raftsmen, some of whom rig out their huge, unwieldy craft with gay streamers, which flutter from the tops of poles. Thus, when several of these rafts are grappled together, forming, as it were, a floating island of timber half a mile wide and a mile long, the sight is extremely picturesque; and when the voices of these hardy sons of the forest and the stream join in some of their Canadian boat songs, the wild music, borne by the breeze along the water, has a charming effect. Myriads of these rafts may be seen lying in the coves at Quebec, ready to be shipped to the different parts of the world.

CANADIAN BOATMEN.

QUEBEC,

until recently the capital of United Canada, is situated on the north shore of the St. Lawrence, in lat. 46 deg. 48 min. north, and long. 71 deg. 15 min. west, from Greenwich. It was founded by Charlevoix, in 1608, on the site of an Indian village, called *Stadacona*. It is the second city in British America, and has a population of more than 45,000. The form of the city is nearly that of a triangle, the plains of Abraham forming the base, and the rivers St. Lawrence and St. Charles the sides. It is divided into two parts, known as the Upper and the Lower Towns. The Upper Town is strongly fortified, and includes within its limits the Citadel of Cape Diamond, which is known to be the most formidable fortress in America. The Lower Town is built upon a narrow strip of land which runs at the base of the cape and of the high ground upon which the Upper Town stands, and the suburbs of St. Roch's and St. John's extend along the river St. Charles and to the Plains of Abraham. Quebec was taken by the British and colonial forces in 1629, but restored to France in 1632; and was finally captured by Wolfe in 1759, and, together with all the French possessions in North America, was ceded to Great Britain at the peace of 1763.

Quebec, including the city and suburbs, contains 174 streets; among the principal of which are the following: — *St. John's Street*, which extends from Fabrique Street to St. John's Gate, in the Upper

CITY OF QUEBEC.

Town, and is occupied chiefly by retail stores; *St. Louis Street* is a handsome and well built street, extending from the Place d'Armes to the St. Louis Gate, and is occupied principally by lawyers' offices and private dwellings; *D'Autueil Street* faces the Esplanade and the ground where the artillery are drilled, and is an elegant street, mostly of private dwellings; *Grand Adlee,* or *St. Louis Road,* outside St. Louis Gate, and leading to the Plains of Abraham, is a pleasant and beautiful street, on which are many elegant villa residences; *St. John's Street,* without, is also a fine street, occupied by shops and private dwellings. The principal street in the Lower Town is *St. Peter's,* on which, and on the wharves and small streets which branch from it, most of the banks, insurance companies, and merchant's offices are situated. There are also several fine streets in the St. John's and St. Roch's suburbs. The appearance of these quarters of the city has been much improved since the great fires of 1845; the buildings that were then destroyed having been replaced by others of a very superior description.

Durham Terrace, in the Upper Town, is a platform commanding a splendid view of the river and the Lower Town. It occupies the site of the old castle of St. Louis, which was burnt in 1834, and was erected by the nobleman whose name it bears.

The Public Garden fronts on Des Currieres street, Upper Town, and contains an elegant monument, which was erected to the memory of Wolf and Montcalm, in 1827. The height of this monument is 65 feet; its design is chaste and beautiful, and no stranger should leave Quebec without visiting it.

The Place d'Armes is an open piece of ground, around which the old chateau of St. Louis, the government offices, the English cathedral, and the court house are situated.

The Esplanade is a beautiful piece of ground, situated between D'Autueil street and the ramparts. It is used as a drill ground by the Royal Artillery.

The Citadel, on Cape Diamond, is one of the most interesting objects to visitors; and those who are desirous of seeing it should make application to the town mayor, at the main guard-house, from whom tickets of admission can always be obtained by persons of respectability. The area embraced within the fortifications of the citadel is more than forty acres.

The line of fortifications, enclosing the citadel and the Upper Town, is nearly three miles in length, and the guns with which they are mounted are mostly thirty-two and forty-eight pounders. There are five gates to the city, three of which, Prescott, Palace, and Hope gates, communicate with the Lower Town, and two of which, St. Louis' and St. John's gates, communicate with the suburbs of the same name. About three quarters of a mile from the city are four Martello Towers, fronting the Plains of Abraham, and intended to impede the advance of an enemy from that direction.

CHURCHES.

The Roman Catholic Cathedral, which fronts upon the Upper Town market-place, is a large and commodious building, but with no great pretensions to architecture. The interior is handsomely fitted up, and has several fine paintings by the old masters, which are well worthy of an inspection. The church will seat 4000 persons. It has a good organ.

St. Patrick's Church, on St. Helen street, Upper Town, is a neat and comfortable building, and is capable of seating about 3000 persons.

St. Roch's Church, on St. Joseph and Church streets, in the St. Roch's suburbs, is a large and commodious building and will seat over 4000 persons. There are several good paintings in this church.

The Church of Notre Dame des Victoires, o.. Notre Dame street, is one of the oldest buildings in the city. It has no pretensions to architectural beauty, but it is comfortably fitted up, and will seat over 2000 persons.

PROTESTANT CHURCHES.

The English Cathedral is situated between Garden street, St. Ann street, and the Place d'Armes, Upper Tov 1, and is a handsome edifice, 135 by 75 feet, and will seat between 3000 and 4000 persons. This church, which was erected in 1804, has a good organ, and is neatly fitted up in the interior.

Trinity Church, situated on St. Nicholas street, Upper Town, is a neat cut stone building, erected in 1824. It is 74 by 48 feet, and the interior is handsomely fitted up.

St. Peter's Chapel is situated on St. Vallier street, St. Roch's, and is a neat plain structure, which will seat about 500 persons.

St. Paul's, or *The Mariner's Chapel*, is a small building near Diamond Harbor, designed principally for seamen.

St. Andrew's Church, in connection with the Church of Scotland, is situated on St. Ann's street, Upper Town. The interior is well fitted up, and will seat over 1200 persons.

St. John's Free Scotch Church is situated on St. Francis street, Upper Town. It is a neat plain structure, and will seat about 600 persons.

The Wesleyan Chapel, on St. Stanislaus street, is a handsome Gothic building, erected in 1850. The interior is well fitted up, and it has a good organ. It will seat over 1000 persons.

The Wesleyan Centenary Chapel is situated on D'Artigny street, and is a plain but substantial edifice.

The Congregational Church, on Palace street, Upper Town, is a neat building of cut stone, erected in 1841, and will seat about 800 persons.

The Baptist Church, on St. Ann street, Upper Town, is a neat stone building, and will seat over 400 persons.

The other principal public buildings worthy of notice are : —

The Hotel Dieu, Hospital and Church, which front on Palace street, Upper Town, and, connected with the cemetery and garden, cover an area of about ten acres. The buildings are spacious and substantial, and the Hospital has beds for about sixty sick.

The General Hospital is situated on the river St. Charles, in the St. Roch's ward. The Hospital, Convent, and Church are a handsome quadrangular pile of stone buildings, well adapted to the purpose for which they are designed.

The Ursuline Convent, situated on Garden Street, Upper Town, was founded in 1641. A number of fine paintings are to be seen here, and application for admission should be made to the Lady Superior.

The University of Quebec fronts on Hope street and the Marketplace, Upper Town. The buildings, which are of massive gray stone, form three sides of a quadrangle, and have a fine garden in the rear.

The Court House and the *City Hall* are substantial stone buildings, situated on St. Louis street, and well adapted to their respective purposes.

The Jail is situated at the corner of St. Ann and St. Stanislaus streets, Upper Town, and is a massive stone building, and cost about £60,000. It is in a healthy location, and well adapted to the purpose for which it was designed.

The Jesuit Barracks front on the Upper Town market-place and St. Ann street. They have accommodations for about 1000 men. A battalion of infantry is usually quartered here.

The Marine Hospital, situated on the river St. Charles, in the St. Roch's ward, is intended for the use of sailors and emigrants, and is a beautiful stone building of four stories. It was erected at a cost of £15,000, and will accommodate about 400 patients.

The Lunatic Asylum is situated at Beauport, two and a half miles from Quebec, and is an extensive building, enclosed in a park of about 200 acres.

The Quebec Music Hall is a handsome cut stone edifice, recently erected, situated on St. Louis street, Upper Town.

The Quebec and Richmond Railroad, connecting the city of Quebec with the Montreal and Portland Railroad. A distance of 100 miles is now completed, not only to point Levi, opposite to Quebec, but it is extended to St. Thomas, a distance of twenty miles below Point Levi.

Among the notabilities of Quebec and its vicinity, is the spot where General Montgomery fell, which is on the road from Champlain street to Diamond Harbor, and is pointed out by a board affixed to the cliff above it.

The Plains of Abraham, a little to the west of the city, where the celebrated battle was fought between the British forces, under General Wolfe, and the French forces, under General Montcalm, should be visited by every traveller. A monument, erected on the spot where General Wolfe fell, points out the place where the hottest part of the action occurred.

Spencer Wood, the former residence of the governor-general, about a mile further west, is an elegant country house.

HOTELS.

Russell's Hotel, Palace street, Upper Town, is an excellent establishment. Mr. Russell spares no pains in promoting the comfort of his guests, and his house affords every accommodation that the most fastidious can desire.

There are also several other excellent houses in the city.

The situation of Quebec, and the scenery all around it, are, at every turn, most beautiful and picturesque. The mountains are tolerably high, and present a fine appearance in the distance. There is a very noble view from the citadel, which, as has been before remarked, is the strongest post in America; and, indeed, next to Gibraltar, Quebec is the strongest fortified place in the world. The view from the citadel is connected with associations of the most interesting character. Here may be seen the Plains of Abraham, where, after his bold ascent of the almost impassable heights from the river, Wolfe appeared in arms at morning dawn, and where Montcalm, with equal courage and gallantry, came out to meet him, though not compelled to do so, and where both heroes fell in the sanguinary struggle of that day, — each a bitter loss to his country, each a living name in the annals of their military glory, and both a brilliant evidence of French and British valor. The memorial of mutual valor here erected is at least an instance of generosity in rivals, which it is pleasant to contemplate. If anything could detract from the horrors of war, it would be instances like this.

The city of Quebec is one which it is impossible to approach without pleasure, and to leave without regret. Every locality connected with the place is fraught with interest to the traveller. As the limits of this work permit only general description, visitors will do well to avail themselves of the small city guides, which they can find at the principal hotels.

THE FALLS OF MONTMORENCI.

In taking our departure from Quebec, and on our way down the river, we pass this celebrated cascade. These falls, which are situated in a beautiful nook of the river, are higher than those of Niagara, being more than two hundred and fifty feet; but they are very narrow, being only some fifty feet wide. This place is a very cele-

FALLS OF MONTMORENCI.

brated focus of winter amusements. During the frost, the spray from the falls accumulates to such an extent as to form a cone of some eighty feet high. There is also a second cone of inferior altitude, and it is this of which visitors make the most use, as being less dangerous than the higher one. They carry "toboggins,"—long, thin pieces of wood,—and having arrived at the summit, place themselves on these and slide down with immense velocity. Ladies and gentlemen both enter with equal spirit into this amusement. It requires much skill to avoid accidents; but sometimes people do tumble heels over head to the bottom. They generally drive to this spot in sleighs, taking their wine and provisions with them; and upon the pure, white cloth, which nature has spread out for them, they partake of their dainty repast, and enjoy a most agreeable picnic. One does not feel in the least cold, as the exercise so thoroughly warms and invigorates the system. The distance of these falls from Quebec is eight miles.

THE CHAUDIERE FALLS,

on the river Chaudiere, nine miles below Quebec, are also a favorite resort, and are very beautiful and romantic. The river here is about four hundred feet wide, and the height of the falls is one hundred and thirty feet.

THE ISLAND OF ORLEANS,

situated in the river St. Lawrence, immediately below Quebec, is nineteen miles long by five and a half miles wide, and, like the Island of Montreal, is superior in fertility to the main land adjacent to it. Its present population is about six thousand.

THE FALLS OF ST. ANNE

are situated on the river of the same name, on the north side of the St. Lawrence, twenty-four miles below Quebec, and present a variety of wild and beautiful scenery, both in themselves and their immediate neighborhood.

LAKE ST. CHARLES,

thirteen miles north of Quebec, is a favorite resort of tourists, particularly of those who are fond of angling, as the lake abounds in fine trout.

GROSSE ISLE

is situated thirty miles below Quebec. Here is the Quarantine Station,— a sorrowful place everywhere; but there is an unusually melancholy interest attached to this one, from the fact that no less than six thousand Irish emigrants were buried in one grave during the terrible year of famine in that country. Apart from these saddening recollections, the island is a fair and agreeable spot, and its scenery is very beautiful. Below this island the river becomes wider and wider, and we soon lose sight of land altogether.

MALBAIE,

ninety miles below Quebec, on the north shore, is a large village, where many of the people of Quebec resort for sea bathing.

KAMOURASKA,

on the south shore, ninety miles below Quebec, is also a thriving village, very pleasantly situated, and resorted to as a bathing place.

RIVIERE DU LOUP, EN BAS,

is situated on the south shore, one hundred and fourteen miles below Quebec, and is a rising village, much frequented for sea bathing.

THE RIVER SAGUENAY

falls into the St. Lawrence from the north, at a distance of one hundred and forty miles below Quebec. This noble river takes its rise in Lake St. John, and has a total length of one hundred and twenty-six miles, till it falls into the St. Lawrence. It is navigable for large vessels sixty miles, and at Ha Ha Bay, fifty miles from its mouth, the largest fleet of men-of-war would find a safe and spacious anchorage. The river is very deep, and at its mouth a line of three hundred and thirty fathoms was thrown without finding the bottom; and at the distance of sixty miles from the St. Lawrence, its average depth is from fifty to sixty fathoms. The shores of this river present some of the grandest and most striking scenery in the world, rising from the water almost perpendicularly to a height of from one thousand to fifteen hundred feet; and in many places a ship of the line might run close to the rocks which overhang it.

TADOOSAC HARBOR

is situated on the northeast side of the river, at its mouth. It is a port of the Hudson's Bay Company, who have a resident and a considerable establishment here.

TETE DU BULE

is a remarkable round mountain, on the north shore, three miles above Tadoosac. A few miles further up are two hills known as the TWO PROFILES, from the strong resemblance which they bear to the human face.

ST. JOHN'S BAY,

twenty-eight miles above Tadoosac, on the south shore, and the mouth of Mackenzie's River on the north shore, are places which contain large lumbering establishments.

ETERNITY POINT AND CAPE TRINITY,

on the south shore, six miles above St. John's Bay, are two immense masses of rock, rising from the water's edge to a height of about fifteen hundred feet, and affording a prospect of solemn and imposing grandeur. STATUE POINT comes next in succession, and then the TABLEAU. This is a perpendicular rock rising to the height of nine hundred feet. The scenery continues very beautiful on to HA HA BAY, which is nine miles in length, and six miles in width, and affords good anchorage for the largest vessels, the average depth being from twenty to thirty-five fathoms.

CHICOUTIRNI

is situated sixty-eight miles above Tadoosac. The Hudson's Bay Company have a post here, and there is a Roman Catholic Church, erected by the Jesuits in 1727. The population is about four hundred, principally French Canadians. The steamboat navigation of the Saguenay ends here, as the river above is obstructed by rapids and falls. Fifty miles above this place is LAKE ST. JOHN, a fine expanse of water of about thirty miles in length, and in the widest part the same in breadth; its superficial area being over five hundred miles.

LAKE ST. JOHN, the SAGUENAY, and the rivers which they receive, abound in excellent fish. The salmon ascends the Saguenay to a considerable distance, and is taken in large quantities and shipped to Quebec.

GEOGRAPHICAL AND STATISTICAL SKETCH OF CANADA.

THE Province of Canada, including both its grand divisions, extends from forty-two to fifty-two degrees of north latitude, and from sixty-four to ninety-two degrees of west longitude, embracing a superficial area of about 330,000 square miles, and having a population of about 2,250,000 souls.

Previous to the year 1791, the whole extent of country now known as Upper and Lower Canada was designated the *Province of Quebec;* but, owing to alleged difficulties in managing the administration of so large an extent of country, it was in that year divided into two provinces, having separate governments, and so remained until 1841, when they were reunited, and now constitute one province only.

Lower Canada, which is considerably the largest province, has an area of 210,000 square miles, and Upper Canada an area of 121,000 square miles; the population being about 1,200,000 in Upper, and 1,100,000 in Lower, Canada.

About two thirds of the population of Lower Canada are of French descent, the remainder consisting of English, Irish, Scotch, Germans, and Americans, or their descendants. In Upper Canada the population is made up of colonists, or the descendants of colonists, from the British Islands; of the descendants of American loyalists who emigrated to Canada after the revolutionary war; and, in a few localities, there are settlements of Germans and Dutch. In Lower Canada about four fifths of the people belong to the Roman Catholic Church, the remainder consisting of members of the different Protestant churches, and a few Jews; while in Upper Canada about four fifths of the people are Protestant, and the remainder Roman Catholic.

At the time of the conquest of Canada, in 1760, the entire population was estimated at 70,000; and a glance at the following synopsis, from the official returns of the different periods mentioned, will show the rapid advance which the country has made since that time.

LOWER CANADA.		UPPER CANADA.	
Population in 1763, ...	70,000	Population in 1763, ...	12,000
" " 1814, ...	335,000	" " 1814, ...	95,000
" " 1823, ...	427,000	" " 1824, ...	151,000
" " 1831, ...	512,000	" " 1832, ...	261,000
" " 1844, ...	609,000	" " 1842, ...	486,000
" " 1848, ...	770,000	" " 1848, ...	721,000
" " 1850, ...	791,000	" " 1850, ...	791,000
" " 1851, ...	890,000	" " 1851, ...	952,000
Estimated in 1854, ...	1,000,000	Estimated in 1854, ...	1,200,000

The total population of Canada, according to origin and religion, by the census of 1852, was as follows:—

Of British origin or descent, in both Provinces, . . . 1,063,743
Of French origin or descent, in both Provinces, . . . 695,945
Of other origin or descent, in both Provinces, ... 82,577
        Total of both Provinces, ... 1,842,265

Protestants in both Provinces, ... 927,253
Roman Catholics in both Provinces, ... 914,561
Jews in both Provinces, ... 451
        Total in both Provinces, ... 1,842,265

a few
Lower
ıtholic
Prot-
about
Roman

popu-
ıg sy-
d, will
; time.

12,000
95,000
151,000
261,000
486,000
721,000
791,000
952,000
200,000

ligion,

33,743
95,945
32,577

12,265

27,253
4,561
451

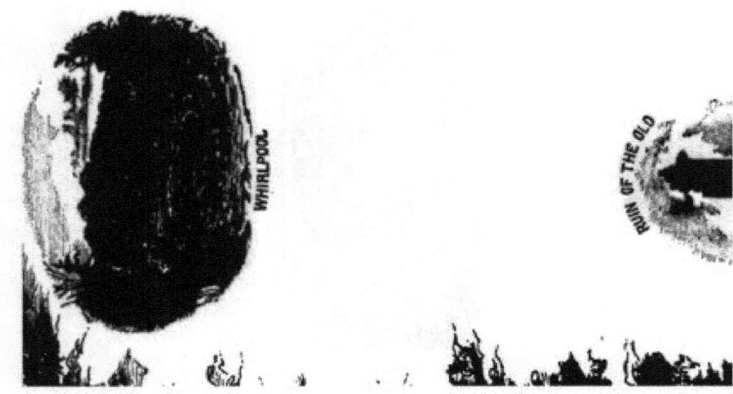

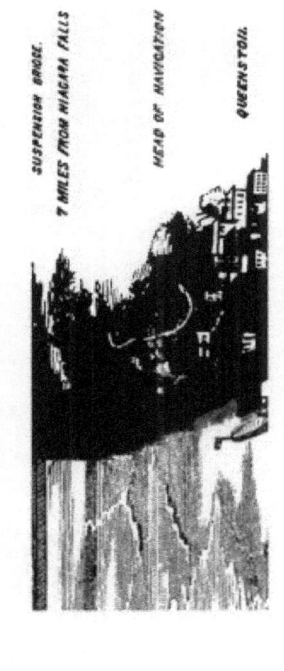

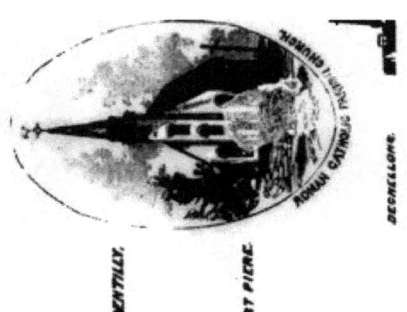

CONTINUED

VAPOR ARE PERFECTLY SALT
FOR A DISTANCE OF
50 MILES BELOW QUEBEC.

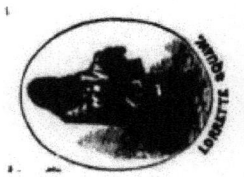

www.ingramcontent.com/pod-product-compliance
Lightning Source LLC
Chambersburg PA
CBHW032244080426
42735CB00008B/998